The Canoe
He Called Loo Taas

The Canoe
He Called Loo Taas

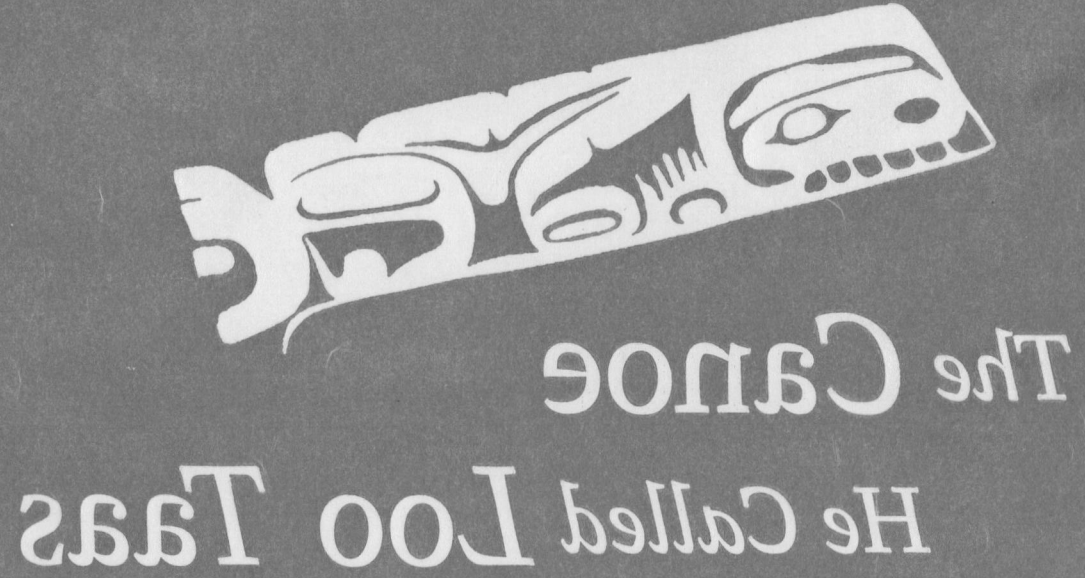

The Canoe
He Called Loo Taas

The Canoe He Called Loo Taas

By Amanda Reid-Stevens
Illustrated by Michael Nicoll Yahgulanaas

BENJAMIN brown books, Ltd.
Vancouver, British Columbia

Copyright © 2010
by Amanda Reid-Stevens

Illustrations Copyright © 2010
by Michael Nicoll Yahgulanaas

All rights reserved. BENJAMIN brown books, Ltd., is a member of Access Copyright. No part of this publication may be reproduced, stored in a retrieval system or transmitted in any form or by any means without prior written permission from the publisher or a license from Access Copyright.

For further information, contact BENJAMIN brown books, Ltd., at #121–3495 Cambie Street, Vancouver, BC, V5Z 4R3. Visit our website at www.benjaminbrownbooks.com

10 11 12 13 14   5 4 3 2 1
FIRST EDITION

Photo on p.18 used by permission of Heather Ramsay/
Queen Charlotte Island Observer.

LIBRARY AND ARCHIVES CANADA CATALOGUING IN PUBLICATION

Reid-Stevens, Amanda
    The canoe he called Loo Taas / Amanda Reid-Stevens, author; Michael Nicoll Yahgulanaas, illustrator.

ISBN 978-0-9782553-6-7

1. Reid, Bill, 1920-1998—Juvenile literature. 2. Loo Taas (Canoe)—Juvenile literature. 3. The Haida Nation/Haida Indians—Boats—Juvenile literature. 4. Canoes and canoeing—Design and construction—Juvenile literature. I. Yahgulanaas, Michael Nicoll II. Title.

VM353.R45 2010   j623.82'9   C2009-906885-0

Printed in China

For K̲uuyas and Juul

BENJAMIN brown books, Ltd., would like to thank The Haida Heritage Centre at K̲aay Llnagaay for their help and support of this project.

"Loo Taas" means
"Wave Eater"
in the Haida language.

ACKNOWLEDGEMENTS

When I really think about it, there are approximately 900 people who had a hand in building this book and every one of them needs to be thanked, so let's get started, shall we?

I'm kidding.

Great big thanks to my editor Tonya Martin and BENJAMIN brown books, Ltd., for performing no little magic in transforming a dog-eared, one-page manuscript into a real, live children's book.

My love, thanks and deep appreciation to Nanaay Binky, Nika, Danny, Walker, Tyson, and Ryde for their kind spirits, ongoing encouragement, and for making me laugh.

I am deeply grateful to Simon Davies who several years ago handed me my first writing assignment and managed not to wince when I told him I was no good with computer stuff.

Many, many thanks to Michael Nicoll Yahgulanaas for his encouragement and taking time out of his outrageously hectic schedule to create the wonderful illustrations for this book.

And last but not least, my sincere thanks to Janna Wilson, Monique Brown, Jason Alsop, Guujaaw, Andy Wilson, and Herb Jones, for their very kind assistance.

Haawa.
— *Amanda Reid-Stevens*

A big canoe named Loo Taas

Was made from a cedar tree –

It took five months to carve her,

And set her in the sea.

Many different people

Worked many days and nights –

Using chisels, knives, and adzes,

They built Loo Taas just right.

Her colour is a deep, rich brown;

She's silky to the touch.

Everyone who knows her

Loves her very much.

Two whale designs are on her hull –

They help her "eat" big waves.

But she's gentle with her passengers –

She never misbehaves.

She's been to many villages,

And once she went to France.

She carries fourteen paddlers

Who sing and drum and dance.

Loo Taas offers her assistance

During happy times and sad.

She cradles little children

And chiefs, and moms, and dads.

Loo Taas glides when she is racing –

She slices through the sea.

She's fast and sleek and beautiful –

On the water she is free.

And when her day is finished,

She slips back to the shore.

Then fourteen paddlers lift Loo Taas,

And guide her through a door.

She sleeps in a Canoe House

In a land called Haida Gwaii.

People often visit her –

Maybe someday YOU'LL stop by!

HEATHER RAMSAY / *Queen Charlotte Island Observer*

AFTERWORD

Loo Taas is a real 50-foot Haida canoe. She was born in the village of Skidegate, Haida Gwaii, with the help of her designer, the late Bill Reid, and a hard-working team of carvers and assistants. Originally commissioned by the Bank of British Columbia (Bank of BC) for Expo '86, she was later gifted to Skidegate by the Hong Kong and Shanghai Banking Corporation Canada (HSBC Canada), and made the trip back home from Vancouver, by water, under the power of a team of young Haida paddlers. Now almost 25 years old, *Loo Taas* is enjoying the company of three big, beautiful, *new* canoes, all of which were unveiled and launched in 2008 during the grand opening of the Haida Heritage Centre at Ḵaay Llnagaay in Skidegate. The first of these canoes is named *The Spirit of Rediscovery*; the second is named *Bears Awakening*; and the third is named *T'aa*.

The *Loo Taas* project, which spanned several months during 1985-86, had a number of training components built into it, and, not surprisingly, turned into a project to which many people from our community — as well as several other communities — generously lent helping hands. It was, overall, a happy and exciting time because, until the work on *Loo Taas* began, a full-size cedar canoe hadn't been carved in Skidegate in approximately 100 years.

There were a number of steps leading up to the creation of *Loo Taas*, the most critical of which was finding the right tree. Herb Jones was the man who didn't give up, and, after six weeks of searching the forest, found the right red cedar. It took a full day for Herb, his son Jim, and the late Larry Vogstad, to make preparations for falling the monumental cedar, which measured approximately 230 feet in height, and nine feet across at the butt. Herb is currently a retired forest worker, and also teaches Haida language to children at the Skidegate Day Care Centre.

A great deal of study and research also took place in preparation for the design of *Loo Taas*. Bill and a young man named Guujaaw worked together on addressing the complexities that required consideration in developing a design for a large, functional, and graceful canoe. Much of the work involved talking with Elders, studying old Haida canoes held in museums, and "back-engineering." Today, Guujaaw is the president of the Council of the Haida Nation as well as an accomplished artist and carver.

When the actual carving of *Loo Taas* began, it wasn't long before the carving shed was regularly visited by people of all ages. There was rarely a day when an Elder didn't stop by to check on the progress, to cheer on the carvers, or to offer suggestions and advice. This deep interest and support was integral to all phases of the project and a large factor in bringing the months of work to a successful conclusion.

In November 2009, *Loo Taas* transported distinguished Elder, Percy Williams, to the shores of K̲aay Llnagaay (Sea Lion Town), where he was greeted by chiefs, drummers, singers, dancers, and a large crowd of cheering spectators representative of all communities of Haida Gwaii. Cameras clicked and cameras rolled as Percy disembarked from the canoe, held high a torch, and commenced his run as an official Olympic torchbearer. And then, oh baby, the crowd went wild!

AMANDA REID-STEVENS

Amanda Reid-Stevens was born in Toronto, Ontario to Mabel (Binky) Stevens and legendary Haida artist Bill Reid. When Amanda's mother later remarried, the family moved to Skidegate, Haida Gwaii and quickly became immersed in the activities of the busy community. Amanda and her late brother, Raymond, who was also an accomplished artist, were raised in Skidegate by their mother and stepfather, Billy Stevens. Billy was a hardworking faller, commercial fisherman, and argillite carver.

Although Amanda lived, at various times, in the lower mainland while attending school and during her first marriage, her heart and home are on Haida Gwaii — it's not an exaggeration to say that she is passionate about her community. Amanda is presently a member of the Haida Gwaii Museum board of directors and has, in the past, served on a number of other boards and committees, including the Coast Sustainability Trust's Haida Gwaii Regional Steering Committee and the board of TRICORP, an Aboriginal capital corporation.

Amanda's employment history is eclectic. She has worked as a grocery store clerk, Band administrator, a baker/seller of homemade cheese biscuits, a secretary, and, for several years, as general manager of Gwaalagaa Naay, Skidegate's economic development corporation. She has also worked as a volunteer proofreader, an executive director for the K̲aay Llnagaay Heritage Centre Society, a baker/seller of one homemade chocolate cheesecake, a Skidegate Band Councillor, a babysitter, and as a trainee in the Council of the Haida Nation's Communications Program. Amanda spends her spare time looking for a better chocolate cheesecake recipe — when she's not doing contract work.

Amanda is a contributing writer to *Haida Laas*, a collection of newsletters and journals published by the Council of the Haida Nation, and was previously a contributing writer to *SpruceRoots Magazine,* an island environmental journal published by the Gowgaia Institute.

Amanda is no stranger to writing in rhyme. Her lifelong interest in writing and rhyming can be credited to her mother, who made sure that Amanda and her brother wrote thank-you letters to off-island relatives each and every time they were sent birthday or Christmas gifts. Amanda quickly learned to make letter-writing more enjoyable by writing in rhyme or creating stories she thought were funny. In her first book, *The Canoe He Called Loo Taas*, Amanda is finally sharing her gift of storytelling.

The Canoe He Called Loo Taas celebrates the true story of a 50-foot Haida canoe made from a single, monumental, red cedar. The canoe was designed by the late Bill Reid and carved in the village of Skidegate by a hardworking team of young carvers. ("Loo Taas," pronounced "loo toss," is a Haida name meaning "Wave Eater.")

Amanda is the loud, proud mom of three grown children — Nika, Walker, and Tyson — and a shamelessly boastful Nanaay (grandma) of two wee granddaughters, Ḵuuyas and Juul.

This is Amanda's first title with BENJAMIN brown books, Ltd.

SKETCH COURTESY OF MICHAEL NICOLL YAHGULANAAS

MICHAEL NICOLL YAHGULANAAS

Was born
and
does live.

SKETCH COURTESY OF MICHAEL NICOLL YAHGULANAAS

www.haidamanga.com

SKETCH COURTESY OF MICHAEL NICOLL YAHGULANAAS

www.haidamanga.com

BENJAMIN BROWN BOOKS

BENJAMIN brown books, Ltd., is an independent, trade children's book publisher located in Vancouver, British Columbia. Please visit our website at: *www.benjaminbrownbooks.com* for more information.

We would like to extend our heartfelt thanks and appreciation to Bob, Bill, Renee, and Daryl. Thank you.

PRINTED & BOUND BY Everbest Printing · DISTRIBUTION (CAN) Publishers Group Canada · FULFILLMENT (USA) Bookmasters Inc. · STOCK Taiwan Superior Ivory (80 lb) · FONT Huronia by Ross Mills/Tiro Typeworks

PUBLISHER Meghan Spong · EDITOR-IN-CHIEF Tonya Martin · DESIGNER Mauve Pagé · AUTHOR Amanda Reid-Stevens · ILLUSTRATOR Michael Nicoll Yahgulanaas